Be Wee With Bea

Learn Ways To Cope

Discover many rigorous exercises
to help you figure out how to
deal with just about any problem

Liz O'Neill

Be Wee With Beat Part 1
Copyright © 2022 Liz O'Neill

Library of Congress Control Number: 2022948862
Paperback: 978-1-958169-66-7
eBook: 978-1-958169-67-4

Contents

Acknowledgement

For nearly 20 years, I taught Creative Writing in grades 6-8. I greatly envied the luxury of writing time my students had. Many of them demonstrated exceptional skill in their compositions. An untold number of them have gone on to become writers; some already published. Some are playwrights or song composers with published recordings. Some have successfully done choreographing entertaining scenarios or stirring sermons to deliver.

I want to thank all of the hundreds of writing students, whose magnificent works have crossed my teacher's desk, for your inspiration.

Hopefully, the teacher has at least matched the student.

About The Author

L iz K. O'Neill, a third generation Vermonter, spent 28 years in a
Religious Community and has a Master's degree in Education with
a Minor in Language Arts. She taught Writing and Literature in grades
6-10 for 20 years. She has written curricula for her undergraduate and
graduate courses in her local college, where she taught for seven years.

At that same time, she volunteered and was later employed for
approximately 30 years in a woman's advocacy shelter, where she
developed an extensive educational website called Imbalance in
Relationships and is, at the time of this writing, a Mental Health
Worker in a psychiatric / substance abuse treatment program. She is
very interested in archaeology,

She has currently completed several books: "Bea Wee With Bea Part
2," working on another part 3 book. She has also completed two other
books: One is called "Traffic," which features the rescue of 10 Native
American Teens from a trafficking operation.

Another called "Tor," featuring power spots in England and deviates to
a time travel vortexing into a monastery in the 16th century.

The last one which she began 20+ years ago, called "A Particular
Friendship," is about her time before entering the Convent, during her
time there, and her life after she has left the Convent.

Dedication

I will be ever grateful to Timothy Fisher who inspired the character of Timothy, the woodcarving, clay pot making, furniture building beaver. Timothy Fisher is an excellent, very skilled wood carver who often exhibits his works in the Middlebury, Vermont area. Tim who is also a proficient writer encouraged me to begin writing in one of my favorite genres, the allegory.

Finally, nearly 20 years later, I have completed his suggestion.

A Note To The Reader

WARNINGS

Are signaled for the reader

By five beaver tail slaps sounded on the water

Reading this book may cause, in no particular order, the following side effects:

1. You may feel compelled to do some or all of the "Bea Wee with Bea" exercise program

2. You may discover yourself dancing in the wind

3. You may feel drawn to explore different paths than you have ever traveled

4. You may find yourself strolling more often than you ever have

5. You may notice that you are losing your appetite for getting into others' business

6. You may find yourself seeking different bodies of water; be they waterfalls, streams, oceans, ponds, lakes or even puddles

7. You may surprise yourself when you find yourself having a sense of humor about your actions or situations

8. You may find yourself being much better able to deal with just about any problem

Introduction

Be Wee With Bea incorporates, without being too obvious, just about every well-known recovery issue. This simply written, book contains both humor and poignancy, operating on a dual level in which both children and adults may gain insight and enjoyment. The main character, Bea the Wee Bear, could easily be any of our own biographical figure.

Much of what she experiences, many of us have experienced. She is a bit of an overeater and a severe sugar addict, who binges on exercise while bingeing on honey, her "be good to myself" treat. Her mother confused nurturing with food. She discovers ways to solve many of her problems with several exercises, one being meditation, which she calls her "Brain Exercise".

Some of the problems she deals with are: being picked on by the little bears in the neighborhood, rescuing an abused cat, an abused puppy, understanding loneliness, and working on honesty in friendships and how not to try to control everything. She has a co-dependent relationship with Scruffles the Raccoon Cat and a homeless puppy. He keeps getting bitten and beaten up by two cat gang members called Briar and Simon. Scruffles and Puppy both had poor self-esteem because of abuse and neglect, as a result of living in an abusive household. Bea chose her own name when her mother wrote out "BEAR" and she dropped a drip of honey on the "R." She encouraged Scruffles to change his name from Scruffy to Scruffles. Bea does have a very healthy friendship with Timothy the Talented Beaver, a wonderful wood carver, furnishing Bea with many nice pieces of furniture and some clay pots in which to store her honey.

So, you see, my book Be Wee With Bea is quite well rounded. I hope I have piqued your interest and you will read on further.

Preface

Timothy, the wood carving, clay pot making, furniture building beaver, who you will meet later, introduced me to Bea the wee bear. I was immediately attracted to her. I felt energized as I joined her in her strolling exercise along Bea's golden path. I met her dear handsome friend Scruffles the Raccoon Cat and Sweet Puppy who are the center of many of Bea's adventures; especially when she learns new things about herself.

I have learned new things about myself from using her suggestion of doing brain exercises to find answers to problems. She didn't even seem to mind that I tracked mud into her home which was an enormous cave with a variety of tunnels branching out in different directions, forming very comfortable rooms. I thoroughly enjoyed watching her do her rigorous exercise program of step-stooling, fine motor weight lifting, toe-touching, and floor-touching. I laughed as she did running-in-place, all to be wee.

Chapter 1

WISHING TO BE WEE

Background

We meet Bea the Wee Bear and see her doing her rigorous exercises to be wee. She feels she has to be wee because she was bullied about her size.

Bea, an unusual name for a wee bear, was the name she had carried since the day she learned how to write. She had, during many of her strolling exercises with her mom, seen names of things written on signs and wondered what her name would look like. She asked her mom to write her name on a piece of paper so she could learn how to write it. Well, she was having a little honey, later to be known as her "be good to myself" treat, and dropped a drip of it right on the "R" at the end of her name. So, licking her yummy right paw and gripping with all of her might, a purple crayon in her left, she copied the letters one after another: B-E-A. You see, her mom hadn't ever quite decided what to name her, so she had always called her Bear. Her mom was so pleased to see that Bea had chosen her own name. She was already beginning the exercise of solving her own problems.

When her mom called outside for her, there was sometimes a bit of confusion because the wrong bee would come. Bea's eyes would glimmer because she didn't really mind. She liked bees because they were the ones who made her "be good to myself" treat.

Every time her mom asked her if she wanted any honey, she'd say that she wasn't hungry, no matter how much her stomach rumbled, grumbled, or growled. Why should she have a "be good to myself" treat when she does not feel good about herself?

Bea frequently had to fight off her bad memories, and she had a lot of them. All her wee life, she'd struggled with the feeling that she needed to work very hard to be wee. It all stemmed from when she was very little and the little mean bears who lived in the forest by her and her mom's cave would bully her about her size.

She knows in her deepest part that she is and has always been a good wee bear. Her mom had told her that over and over many, many times, but still, it was hard not to remember the voices, which stuck like honey, of those mean little bears yelling and yelling. She said she thought if she did rigorous exercises often enough, it would make the voices go away.

Bea knew that her mom loved her and her friends accepted her just the way she was, but sometimes she felt like giving up when the little bears yelled "No fat bears" every time she came around to play. She was sure if she were wee, maybe they would have invited her to play. She decided that she just wouldn't eat anymore. After so many mean bears had said bad things to her and about her so many times and for so long, Bea had begun to believe them. She believed those little bears must be right because how could that many of them be wrong? It must be true.

She never counted how many there were, but it felt like a lot. It had always been a very painful blur in her memory.

She had stopped drawing on paper and wrote all over her fur with different colored crayons. She had always hoped that she could become invisible so the mean bears wouldn't know she was around. But then there were times when she didn't want to be invisible, but she was. Maybe she'd wished too hard and things got out of balance. Being invisible turned out to be as painful as being visible. When she was invisible, no one seemed to see how sad she was or how she was being treated. She would go somewhere else in her head. Maybe her thoughts could do some kind of magic and make her a good wee bear instead of a bad fat bear.

She wanted to tell her mom how horrible she felt inside but didn't know where to start. Her mom saw how very sad and hurt Bea was and told Bea she did not have to be mean to herself because others were cruel to her. Bea was so surprised that her mom knew some of what was going on without having to say a word. It made it easier. She still didn't say anything.

Reassuring her with a great big bear hug that she was a good wee bear, her mom told her it was time for her to learn to talk to the maker, who passes on to us all the wisdom we need. She taught her how to both talk and listen to the maker of wee bears. When Bea told the maker of wee bears how hard she was wishing to be wee, she heard an idea of how to be wee and still enjoy her "be good to myself" treat: a rigorous exercise program. This was the first of Bea's many wonderful brain exercises. A very satisfied wee bear, she decided to call it "Be Wee with Bea."

The "Be Wee with Bea" rigorous exercise program will cost you nothing. She uses things found right in her home. You can too. She didn't need to go out and buy an expensive exercise machine. She gets the same kind of exercise going up and down her stepstool to get her pots of honey that are up high on shelves, which requires stretching the ribs. This might even prevent Bea from shrinking, as they say people do. The part that makes this a rigorous exercise is that she doesn't do this just a few times or for just a few minutes; she carries on this activity many, many times all day long and sometimes into the wee hours of the night.

She is so dedicated that often she wakes up and realizes that she hasn't done her stool stepping for a while. She gets right up without hesitation or reluctance. This exercise has an added bonus that the store-bought exercise machine doesn't. She is also doing fairly heavy weightlifting, as the pots are brimming full as she lifts and carries them slowly down her steps.

The weights being lifted as she does the going down part are, of course, heavier than they are for the going up part on the stool stepper. This graduated weight program may be a bit backward. Usually, the weights are increased rather than decreased as the program progresses, but Bea knows it will have good effects on her confidence and self-esteem anyway. She realizes that her tummy has a bit of a full feeling, so it's probably just as well that the honeypots are empty and don't weigh very much. Her strength might decrease as her tummy gets fuller.

Once, she got so excited about this exercise program that while she was rushing her fine motor weight lifting -- which simply means having a big pawful of her "be good to myself" treat -- she dropped a drip on her toes. That was when she discovered another exercise, which she calls "toe touching," which of course balances out the full tummy and a bending exercise. Another similar exercise, but one that calls for a wee more stretching, is floor touching.

Sometimes floor touching can develop into running in place if the weights get too tippy and fall on the floor and her feet get all stuck up in this exercise. She may try to use her paw to clean off the honey covering her feet, but if this does not work, she will use it as an opportunity to do some of her dance exercises.

Timothy, the wood carving, clay pot making, furniture building beaver, whom you will meet later, introduced me to Bea the wee bear. I was immediately attracted to her. I felt energized as I joined her in her strolling exercise along Bea's Golden Path. I met her dear, handsome friend Scruffles the Raccoon Cat and Sweet Puppy, who are the center of many of Bea's adventures, especially when she learns new things about herself.

I have learned new things about myself from using her suggestion of doing brain exercises to find answers to problems. She didn't even seem to mind that I tracked mud into her home, which was an enormous cave with a variety of tunnels branching out in different directions, forming very comfortable rooms. I thoroughly enjoyed watching her do her rigorous exercise program of step stooling, fine motor weight lifting, toe touching, and floor touching. I laughed as she did running in place, all to be wee.

After doing her exercises for so many summers, Bea began to notice that she didn't do her vigorous exercises for the same reasons anymore. She somehow knew her exercises were helping her in other ways to solve her problems.

Chapter 2

THE DANCE

She hears them singing their stories of the journey they've been on for hundreds and hundreds of years. Rolling, smoothing their sharp edges; they teach Bea about the struggles in her life. Solving her problems one at a time will help her smooth out and become calmer, allowing her to appreciate everything around her. This will lead her to thank the maker of everything.

She loves to listen to the water sing. Doing her noticing exercise helps her be able to hear that the singing is different almost every day and in different kinds of water. There is a drumming sound when the water is falling from up high. She does a different dance here, drumming with her feet. She does a swishing dance when the water makes a swishing sound. In areas where the water is very still, she just stands there quietly, swaying back and forth and doing her simply enjoying life exercise.

The water, no matter where it is or how it is flowing, sings a special song to Bea about solving her problems. Doing her notice exercise she can see that the water goes around and over the rocks. A lot of the sparkling, glistening, sun-reflecting water just goes around the rocks. It adjusts to the obstacles in front of it. Bea always wants to do this but finds it difficult; which is why she does her brain exercise so often.

She realized at that moment that she had kind of acted like a bully with her problems. She supposed that sometimes that was a good exercise, but maybe not always. Maybe she could learn to bend like water. That was it. Wasn't it? The water kind of bends around the rocks and stuck logs. It definitely needs to bend around the logs in Timothy's Dam, which he worked so hard on for days and days.

She began to do her brain exercise right then. She wondered how her friends really felt when she tried to force a problem to come out the way she thought it should, not the way the maker knew would be best. When she was putting her nose in the wrong place, it usually ended up being a sorry nose, and she would find herself and her nose just plain stuck.

She just had to learn to move on from her planning and scanning. Others and their problems, all too often seemed like just another exercise for her. Something to take her away from her bad memories and bad feeling about herself. She knew she had to begin to be serious about doing her detachment from things that have a hold on your exercise.

She kind of knew how upset, hurt, and discouraged Timothy would be if the water acted like a bully and pushed all of his logs out of the way and rushed through everything he had worked on. The beautiful, strong Timothy's Dam would be demolished even before he'd had time to finish it. Bea thought that maybe she was pushing through her friends' exercise of working on solving their problems before they even finished. Maybe she should wait until they ask her for help. But what if they never asked? Then what would she do? That would be very hard.

She was so used to rushing in to help her mom with every little thing. Because her father was never around, someone had to help. Remembering back, she realized, her mom was trying to tell her she needed to figure her problem out without Bea sticking her nose into everything. Her mom never said it that way, but Bea now understands. But this was a long-term exercise for Bea. This was another lesson she could learn from the song the water sang.

The water teaches Bea how to be safe too. Sometimes, when the water is acting like the little bears that were mean to her when they would bully her, the rough waters sing of danger. Just as she stayed away from them, Bea stays away from that kind of water, which sings a song to remind her to take care of herself.

Bea, the swirling bear, can be seen spinning with her arms spread out as far as they can be when she listens to the breeze going through the trees. She doesn't know for sure if it is the wind singing or the leaves, but she loves how it makes her feel. Just as with the water, it is different every day and sometimes from moment to moment.

Bea felt a bit of a twinge as she had a bad memory of what happened when she was little and the wind barely had time to sing of danger to her mom and the large elm tree came crashing down on their cave, gouging a very large hole in their home. She still practiced her on-alert exercise when the wind began to change its song to a faster, deeper whistling sound. If that all-too-familiar song continued for too long, and she could feel her fears growing with the strength of the bully-like wind, Bea did her sprinting exercise and got out of there as fast as she could.

Oh, but the birds—yes, the birds. What beautiful songs they sing. When Bea does her noticing exercise, she hears so many different sounds. Some even seem to be dancing on the thin branches, causing the branches with leaves and pine boughs to dance also. Bea can't help but join them with her dance exercise.

Sometimes the song the wind, leaves, water, or birds sang, matched how Bea was feeling. The woeful moaning song helped her do her noticing exercise. She never wanted to burden her friends with her sadness or anger. She preferred to be still, like the calm water. She didn't feel so alone with her feelings of loss when she heard the mourning dove or the wind sing the song that was in her heart as she thought of her wonderful time with Timothy and how much she missed her mom. She also missed the happy times at play that she felt the mean little bears took away from her by not allowing her to play with them.

She often wondered in her brain exercise what things would have been like if her father had been around more and if she could really have had the courage to tell her mom what those mean little bears were doing to her and how they were treating her. She realized that was one of the main reasons she started to pretend. She didn't really want to have to pretend, but that seemed to be the only way she knew how. She had to pretend that she didn't really mind that her father was never there. She didn't want to hurt her mom's feelings. She needed to take care of her.

She wondered if she'd learned to pretend from her mom, who never said a bad word about the fact that her father was so absent. When Bea would do her noticing exercise, she could see great sadness in her mom's loving eyes. Maybe that was one of her mom's exercises, which had become her own too. But her mom did a good job at pretending.

She taught Bea how to take care of others' feelings by not letting them know how you really feel. Mom still laughed and played with Bea and had her join in her dance exercise and her strolling exercise every day. She even showed Bea all of the good paths where all of the best berries were, and even an occasional pile of nuts saved by the squirrels when no one was at home. She pointed out her favorite streams to catch fish.

But, of course, the best are the places to get honey. Her mom warned her, though, that if she stuck her nose into the yummiest of places, she must be ready to get her nose stung at least once and sometimes many times. But to Bea, it sounded very worth it. That exercise, as you have heard, has taught her many lessons over the years.

Every once in a while, some angry memories would sneak in. Bea knew it was time for her to go stand at the edge of the swirling, frothy waters. It was a mystery to Bea, why this made her feel so calm; but it does. She suspects it has something to do with the maker.

So, Bea does have music when she dances. It is all of these songs that she carries in her heart.

Chapter 3

A LESSON IN BLACK

Bea's mother was teaching her how to gather honey from certain trees. That determined bear was doing her best to pay very close attention. She was cautioned to notice which bees she could and shouldn't go near. Her mom warned her there were some mean bees that didn't look like the kind ones. The mean ones had black near their heads. The bees that gave them honey for the "Be Good to Bea" treat had brown near their heads.

Bea learned black didn't always mean trouble. There were many nice black bears who did not cause any more problems than any other bears. However, there were times she knew to practice her on-guard exercise when she saw black. A black sky meant she and her mom, or anyone else she might be with, needed to get into a safe cave. A group of trees would not do. She learned this from a scary experience when she was little.

She and her mom had planned to do their strolling exercise, which turned into a run for their lives two times in one day. The trouble began when they reached the middle of a broad, treeless field. This was a vulnerable location to be when the sky turned black and there was thunder and lightning. Bea froze when her mother told her to wait until she spotted a safe area. After a sharp inspection, her mom recognized they were surrounded by a metal fence, another "no."

Finally, there were groups of trees reaching outward and upward, as if to catch the lightning. She and her mom did not know what to do. There was absolutely no safe way out of this terrifying situation. Being in the middle of the field, near a fence, and/or under trees was dangerous. The responsible mom bear was driven to protect both fragile Bea and herself. She did not want them to be singed bears. There had to be a safe place around them.

Bea watched in awe as her mom twirled in a hypnotic circle, searching for anywhere they could run to be safe. Trees blurred, and fences wavered as the angry wind picked up force. When that sharp-eyed mom saw it, she had to yell over the rattling and tapping of the downpour for Bea to hear her. It soon became obvious that Bea had heard nothing and may not even have seen her.

Bea had made herself as wee as she could, so she did not see her mom's frantic gestures to run in the direction of the wooden building off in the distance. Granted, it was still under a stand of trees, but it was a shelter from the soaking dampness. Bea was startled when her mom nudged her furry back. At first, she feared she'd been struck by lightning. She'd seen trees that had been stuck down the middle and split apart, revealing the darkness they had hidden. It was right in the middle of her back, too, just like the tree. When her mom put her kind face in front of Bea's, seeing her eyes filled with terror, she gave her a huge hug.

Having gotten Bea's attention and pulled her out of her trance, where she definitely felt beside herself, her mom took her paw. With her new-found courage, Bea followed her mom into the wooded area until she stopped. In front of them stood a wooden building. Her mom cautiously peeked through each of the dusty windows to ensure it was safe for them to temporarily enter. She wasn't sure she should tell Bea what she saw hanging on the dark walls.

She began to tremble when she spied what was hanging over the couch—the color of dirt. Oh well, she had to get in there regardless. Her one question was whether she should tell Bea ahead of time what she saw or just wait 'til they got in there. Bea's caring mom did decide to at least alert her to the fact there were some extremely disturbing sights inside, and whatever she was feeling was real and okay. The clever and considerate mom bear removed the large screen as carefully as she could, so as not to do any major damage to it. This would be ideal for them to crawl through to get away from the dankness. It had to be drier inside, despite the evidence of several massacres occurring. Wee Bea was able to leap through the opening, but her mom was slightly slower, which meant she was not there for Bea when she would have needed her most. By the time her mother arrived, Bea had already seen what her mom dreaded her seeing. The shocked, wee bear stood there, nearing collapse, her eyes filled with horror. She'd never seen anything like that. Her mom feared that Bea would never be able to unsee such a soul-searing sight. The scar of this dark moment would be with her for a lifetime.

In addition to the heads of cousins hanging—around the room, Bea's eyes fell on the killing sticks, brown with another black stick coming from it. She suspected the most dangerous part was the black part. Her mom told her they were called guns, and they shot out tiny pieces of something like stones, but they hurt more than any pebble. She warned Bea to hide as fast as she could if she ever saw a human with one.

There was a strange noise outside that did not sound like normal thunder but more like a growling thunder. The sound of a log crashing to the ground was followed by the sound of feet stomping on the front porch. The sad tone within that dark room quickly morphed from the black mood they were in to an instant need for alertness and escape. Bea wondered what could happen next; she was worn out from the events thus far.

Fortunately, her wise mom had removed the screen from the rear window. If they hurried, they could get back out to the trees. There was no time to replace the screen. The horrible human would have to replace the screen and spend time investigating why it was removed. By then, Bea and her mom would be far away from that danger.

The sun was back out, so they could continue their strolling exercise. Somehow it wouldn't be the same, though. Nothing would ever be the same. We will see later how Bea dealt with more lessons in black as a grown wee bear.

Chapter 4

NO ONE CARING

On one of her rigorous strolling exercises, Bea the wee bear met up with a very unkempt-looking cat who introduced himself as Scruffy. That name certainly suited him, as his fur was all matted and stuck up with some sort of goo. He explained that his owners had children who were never told by their mom to wash their hands or faces. And whenever they touched him or nuzzled their faces into his fur, they left clumps of something sticky on him, like lollipops or ice cream. He had given up on trying to stay clean. Even though cats were supposed to have very strong tongues, his got very tired and very, very sticky.

When Bea did her noticing exercise, she could see how Scruffy's ribs showed through his sad-looking, clumped-up, matted hair. She thought to herself that she would not have to ever worry that her ribs were showing. Then she caught herself and realized she was talking negatively about herself like those mean bears did. She did not want to do that anymore. She brought her attention back to when Scruffy was saying that his favorite food had become the pizza crust. When Bea looked puzzled, he continued to explain how it was the food left from what the kids dropped on the floor under the table. He found himself hanging out a lot down there. He had to be careful not to also bite into some strange object or moldy food stuck to the floor when he was gobbling up the good stuff. He ate when the kids ate, which didn't seem to be very often. So, he spent a lot of time going from door to door and from garbage can to garbage can.

He told Bea that his owners had many, many problems. The kids' dad drank a lot of something in a lot of bottles and a lot of cans. This made him change quickly from fun to very scary—an unsafe place for Scruffy to be around. The angry man would kick at poor Scruffy; one time he almost kicked Scruffy down the long, steep set of stairs. He had had some practice flying; the little girl used to fling poor Scruffy down the stairs almost daily. But to be kicked down was another thing altogether.

Scruffy knew this was what the very sad little girl must have thought would help and found some fun in throwing him down the stairs and watching him fly. He could put up with that; after all, cats can land on their feet and be kind of OK. But this man, who teetered around and bumped into things and threw pizza boxes, was too much for Scruffy.

Bea asked him where the mom was during all of this, and Scruffy said that she was rushing around trying to get the kids out of the way and trying to calm the man down. She didn't have much time for the kids because she was busy worrying about whether the man was going to drink another can of that bad stuff. She cried a lot and just sat around watching TV. The kids would say they were hungry or needed something, and she acted as if she couldn't hear them.

Scruffy said he hoped he was a comfort to them as they petted him with their dirty, sticky hands and hugged and nuzzled his soft hair with their gooey, smudged faces. He said he felt so conflicted. He knew he should stay there for them, but he couldn't take it anymore and needed to take care of himself. He did miss them already and hoped they would be able to find their way through life. But he had to be out of there.

Bea was quickly doing her brain exercise, knowing this was a time to learn something about her own way of living. She could never have heard enough ideas about taking care of herself. She sometimes had the same problem. She told Scruffles about her detachment from things that have a hold on you exercise. He said he would do that exercise and was hoping they would meet again. He thought he could learn a lot from Bea.

Chapter 5

SHARING WITH OTHERS

Bea the wee bear realized that this problem was bigger than she. This caring wee bear was determined to help her new friend find hope. He was scared and lonely. She could not leave him in this terrible situation. Putting all thoughts of her rigorous strolling exercise aside, Bea moved a distance away from Scruffy to begin her brain exercise, which simply meant a very rigorous thinking time away from distractions while she worked on figuring out an answer to a problem. Bea knew if she invited him to be a guest in her home, there would be difficult times, but they could take it one step at a time. She did, however, quickly take a mental inventory of her supply of honey—did she have enough to share?

When the answer came up "yes," she invited Scruffy to live with her. He had no reason to go back, so he accepted her invitation. Bea, this wee kind bear, told Scruffy that his dish would never be empty again. She did her best to help him get some of the snarls out and clean him up a bit. This wise bear knew that after living by herself for so long, she needed to watch her fears, which at times like these snuck in—fears that she wouldn't have enough of everything to be able to share, especially her "be good-to myself" treat. Finally, practicing her notice exercise, Bea realized Scruffy didn't even want to take all of her honey; he didn't even like honey. Still, there was a need for her to do her on-guard exercise.

This was her old way of dealing with the fears she used to get when any sharing had to be done with her brother and sister. When they would begin arguing over who got the most, her mom would tell them they would have to measure or count everything out equally. But now, her mom wasn't around to help; she had died a few years earlier. Bea hadn't felt this way in a long time and didn't like it very much. It was time to do the brain exercise that her mom had taught her.

Bea remembered that the maker of the bees had taken care of things in the past. She quieted herself the way her mom had shown her and began to talk to the maker of the bees, telling him of her fears. There was a buzzing, as if fifty bees were flying around inside her. After a few quiet minutes, she heard a nice, comforting hum in the air—busy bees making honey—and she knew things would work out for both her and Scruffy.

But we all know that sharing does not always go smoothly. As you might have guessed, Bea was doing a little bit of her pretend exercise in her imagination. And her imagination was very strong—as strong as the dam in Timothy's Pond. It was not until reality hit her square in the face that this wee one had to search for the courage to be honest with herself. At first, Scruffy was content to hang out in the cave because, as promised, after accompanying Bea to the nearby babbling brook to catch fish, he had more than he could eat. His tummy was not used to so much food and so rich a meal. Ever.

Bea would have done well to do her noticing exercise and listen to the song the brook was singing. If she had, the message of chaos and confusion would have been heard. But, instead, Bea was busy thinking about how happy she was making Scruffy.

The first night ever that Scruffy had been able to just relax and enjoy his life, he couldn't. He was so restless. Bea, of course, was tired and wanted peace and quiet. She was just not used to this.

Rudely awakened, she heard the strangest sound there'd ever been. It grated terribly on her ears and her nerves. It seemed to be coming from right beside her. It was! Scruffy was yowling, not meowing in the same sweet way as when they first met. Not the contented purring found to be so rewarding for her labors; not of his satisfaction when he was enjoying the fish that Bea had caught for him. NO. It was a very loud and annoying yowl. Bea could have none of this. She promptly scooped him up, much like her mom had in her frenzy to get them to safety. But this was for an entirely different purpose. Bea needed to sleep.

She did a quick brain exercise—clearly not thorough enough of an exercise, as we will soon see. After setting Scruffy down in a far back room, the sleepy ruffled bear returned to her still warm and comfortable leaf and grass bedding. That solution brought far worse results. Just as the lightning flash during storms illuminated every wall in the cave, the cat's yowling was bouncing off, reverberating from every room in the entire cave home.

Bea could stand it no longer. He had to go. She stormed to the back of the cave, into the room that was the loudest. Swiping Scruffy between her very angry paws—thankfully, no claws were used—she proceeded to remove him from the home Bea had so generously offered him. It could be called an "evening eviction." She set him down, in not such a gentle manner, and said nothing more.

Actually, if she had taken time to do her noticing exercise, there would have been a realization that she hadn't spoken a word that entire time, nor remembered to breathe throughout that whole incident. Without much delay, Bea returned to the spot where a wee bear easily falls asleep. This happened without any of her "be good to myself" treats, contrary to what one might expect.

While preparing to do her talk to the maker exercise, as she did to begin every bear day, she had a bad memory. This was not about when she was young but about last night. There was a great need for her to do her brain exercise to understand what had happened. What had she done? Then it hit her. It struck even harder after Bea did her humble exercise. The sad bear remembered how she had acted.

Poor Scruffy. She had acted like a bully toward him. Bea realized there was no difference between her and the mean little bears or the people Scruffy had lived with. How must he feel? Bea knew how she felt. Horrible. She had to find him.

Chapter 6

FIXING CONSEQUENCES

There was no time for her "Be Wee With Bea" rigorous exercise program on the stool stepper; no weightlifting, graduated or otherwise. There would be no fine motor weightlifting, toe touching, or even floor touching. She felt so stuck now, as if she were running in place, going nowhere. She just couldn't seem to make progress. It was a very different kind of stuck. She had to find Scruffy.

She sprinted from room to room of the cave. Even with all her fear growing and the fifty bees buzzing around inside her, she was able to do a noticing exercise. For the first time at that moment, she realized how very, very vast her cave was, or at least that it certainly seemed very expansive right now. He was nowhere to be found. Where could he have gone? Was she so much worse than his family that he would prefer to go back to sitting under the table on the dirty floor, waiting for a piece of pizza crust to drop from the children's grubby hands?

She decided she'd start doing her investigation exercise, looking for Scruffy on all the paths that would be familiar to him. Ah, the first might be where she met him. She sprinted to that now very empty spot and down to the brook, where they had gone earlier yesterday to catch fish for the hungry boy.

You will later learn about why she would want to stop to visit Willow and who Willow was. But for now, it is enough to know that Bea had a wonderful friend who would always be there with undivided attention for her. At this point, she felt like thrashing and crying. Willow had always helped many feel better by just listening. And Bea was absolutely certain Willow would be able to help. For some reason, just knowing she'd be there for Bea helped her do her remain calm exercise, which she knew she should have used last night when she evicted Scruffy.

She decided that she could wait to see Willow and stop to see if Timothy, her beaver friend, was anywhere to be found. If not, then she'd go see Willow. She was closer to where he was. Even though she hadn't eaten and her tummy was probably quite empty, she did her sprinting exercise, hoping to hear the reassuring slap sound on the water. To their agreement, she would slap the water two times so he would know it was her and not some predator. And he'd answer with one slap. As she came nearer Timothy's Pond, her fears started growing. What if Timothy wasn't in his lodge? She stood there with her "if only's" and "why's" and "no, it can't be's." Then she made her courage bigger than her fears and sounded two loud slaps on the water. She was waiting and waiting. Had she done her noticing exercise, she would have realized that it had been a long time since she had taken a breath. Terrible silence. There was no sound of water being slapped by Timothy the Beaver.

Finally. Always finally. When all else fails, Bea remembers to talk to the maker of everything—beavers, cats, and best of all, wee bears. When she heard the gentle slapping of water, she knew somehow things would work out. This and the buzzing of bees always reassured Bea. It felt safer for her to wait in the silence and wait and be calm without trying to force a problem to come out the way she thought it should—not the way the maker knew would be best.

Then she heard Timothy the Beaver's tail slap once on the water. She sounded two slaps, and there was Timothy swimming right to the edge of the pond. She was so relieved. Surely, he'd know what she could do. At first, she was hesitant to tell him the whole story and how she had acted. But then she remembered how understanding he was about so many of her limitations. So, she told him everything that had happened and was as honest as she could be about how she had reacted; she didn't even blame Scruffy for her behavior. Even though it was hard not to give him a little blame, she didn't. Then she sadly mumbled that she wasn't sure she deserved to have a friend like Scruffy. Timothy told her that she did deserve to have such a friend as Scruffy. He offered some good suggestions about what she could do. They made a lot of sense to Bea, but she was pretty sure it would mean a lot of work on her part. She had to be ready to do more hard work, but she knew that the maker would always be there to help.

If she would leave Scruffy's bowl full of fish outside the cave and wait for him, he would come back because he knows Bea cares for him. But that was easy. The hardest part would be that she needed to be humble and let Scruffy say what he wanted. When Timothy asked Bea if she had asked Scruffy what he wanted, she had to admit to him that she hadn't even thought of doing that.

Bea was hoping Timothy could save her from that painful part. But he said he did not know what Scruffy would want; only Scruffy could answer that question. She thanked him very much for helping and remembered to ask him how he was doing. He said he was doing very well. They said goodbye to each other, and Bea was on her way to follow Timothy's suggestions.

She stopped by her favorite fishing spot to get lots of fish for Scruffy's bowl to be set outside. She placed his yummy-smelling bowl at the mouth of the cave, then poised herself in a get-ready spot. She was practicing her alert but calm exercise. More waiting. It seemed lately all she did was wait. It did seem like such a senseless exercise, but she knew it was necessary, as were all waitings, if the desired results were deemed worthwhile enough. Bea felt very strongly that this was worth it. As it grew darker, Bea was losing hope. Doing her talk with the maker of hope made waiting tolerable.

There was no buzzing of bees or gentle slap on the water that followed— only the scraping sound of Scruffy the cat moving the bowl of fish as he ravenously ate. Maybe this was Bea's only chance. Instead of Scruffy springing, it was Bea as she skittered Scruffy and his bowl into the cave. As she did this, in the same breath, she spouted out that she was wrong. It was so wrong the way she had treated him, and she wanted to start over if he would have it that way.

During their discussion, which was very brief, Scruffy said that he needed more freedom. He was not used to being in any one place for very long. He slept with each of the children on their sheetless mattresses. He couldn't stay long with the youngest because his diaper smelled too awful, even for a garbage-rummaging scruffy raccoon cat. He admitted he could eventually get very used to this way of life. It was just going to take some time, and Bea needed to give him that time.

Chapter 7

CARING ABOUT OTHERS

Scruffy began to eat better. In addition to being adept at retrieving honey from bees' hives, bears are also good at catching fish. Scruffy finally dared to tell Bea that he would much rather have fish than honey or some old, hard piece of pizza crust like he was forced to eat in his last home. He began to look a lot better, too. And as time went on, he began to feel a lot better about himself.

During one of her brain exercises, Bea thought about how the name Scruffy made her feel. It reminded her of that scruffy, scrawny cat she met on one of her rigorous strolling exercises. He was nowhere to be found. In his place was a handsome raccoon cat who had the most beautiful fur and a flowing tail that looked like the mane of some of her horse friends. It was time for him to change his name. She thought of a name that would be much more dignified: Scruffles, the Raccoon Cat. It was set; from now on, he would be known as Scruffles, the Raccoon Cat.

Just because Scruffles felt better, it did not, unfortunately, mean that everything around him got better. Sometimes Bea would hear him crying in his sleep and watch his little legs beating back and forth as if he were trying to get away from something. His bad memories had come back ever since the two meanest cats you could ever meet began showing up.

Orian, an ugly orange tomcat, outweighed Scruffles by at least eight pounds. Scruffles had put on some weight by now, but he still weighed only twelve pounds. Bea was afraid he was no match against such a massive cat. Scruffles did surprise her, though. After a terrible battle, she found only one clump of Scruffles' fur on the ground and counted three blond clumps of Orian's hair on his strong, broad back.

From then on, Orian didn't seem as interested in fighting Scruffles. He went back to fighting squirrels, where he had much more success. The more terrible of the two was Sam, who didn't seem to fear anything. His teeth were very, very sharp and could dig deep into Scruffles' back and tail.

Whenever he saw Sam, poor Scruffles just froze. Bea knew that her friend could not handle things on his own and that she needed to do a rigorous brain exercise.

Chapter 8

RESCUING OTHERS

B ea remembered why bears are able to catch fish: they like to splash in the water. But cats? She did not remember ever seeing any cat splashing in the water, as much as they love the "be good to themselves" treat of fish. So, she knew what she would do to stop that mean cat in his wet tracks. Every time he came by to bother Scruffles, she would throw a pot of water—certainly not honey—on him. With excitement and hopes that her plan would work, she gathered her empty honeypots, filled them with water, and placed them in a get-ready spot.

Every time Scruffles was sunning himself, she would stand by, doing her on-guard exercise, holding her wee bear breath, watching and waiting for Sam to show his sinister Siamese self. After several minutes had passed with no sign of Sam, Bea realized she hadn't taken a breath and that she needed to remember to be alert but relaxed.

She was ready with a filled pot when a slinking shadow caught her cautious eye. She splashed him full force with the first of many pots lined up in a row. Boy, did he tear out of there in a big hurry! She thought that was the end of it, surely. Now she could really relax, and Scruffles could return to doing one of the things he did best, lying in the sun.

She couldn't believe her wee bear eyes, which got very big when she saw the stunned or just stubborn Siamese standing right over Scruffles. This time, her throw got Scruffles a little wet but sent that rambunctious cat back under his porch. Bea later found out that Scruffles loved water. He was not afraid to stand over a slightly frozen puddle and attempt to crack it open to get to the water. He would be so focused on this exercise that he didn't seem to care if he became covered with about half an inch of snow.

Bea, now a little skeptical at the results of a cat being splashed with water, needed to make sure that Sam was back where he belonged. When she found him lying so innocently at rest, she felt reassured and headed back to enjoy the sun with Scruffles. It didn't take long for her to discover a new exercise—not rigorous strolling but very rigorous running for your life.

She felt a hot little breath on the back of her legs. Ever so slowly peeking around, she saw Sam about to nip at her wee bear heels with those very sharp pointy teeth of his. Swiftly skittering to safety, she began to do her brain exercise. Once again, she had come upon a problem too big for her to handle alone.

Chapter 9

THE ANSWER

Sometimes, the answer to a problem came to Bea by recalling what had worked in the past. This situation reminded her of the time when there was no honey to be found. The bees just didn't seem to be making it fast enough for her needs. She knew she certainly couldn't make the honey herself, as much as she'd like to be able to. She had that same desperate feeling now; no matter how hard she tried, she just couldn't make things work out right.

She couldn't get the awfully scary cat, Sam, to stay away. She'd tried many things, but nothing had worked. In times past, she had done her talk to the maker exercise—the maker of the bees. She figured the one who made the bees could get the bees to make more honey, so she could be sure she always had enough of her "be good to myself" treat. So, she knew she had to do her talk to the maker exercise.

When she did her listen to the maker exercise, she heard a peaceful, reassuring buzz in the air and knew that the maker of the bees had heard her request. She decided she'd take a risk and ask the maker of the bees about this problem. After all, the maker of the bees was also the maker of the cats. As she did her listen to the maker exercise, there was a stillness in the air, which told her to be still inside. She knew that somehow things would work themselves out without her help.

A very pleasant and peaceful week had passed before she realized that she had not seen any sign of Sam. She knew he would not return. She did not know where he had gone, but she did not question the ways of the maker of the bees, the maker of the cats, and best of all, the maker of the wee bears.

Often, while basking in the warm sun, as cats love to do, Scruffles would tell Bea how wonderful his life with her was and how safe and happy he felt now. Listening to Scruffles talk about his sad times had started Bea remembering what it was like when she was little. Her father was away a lot, gathering honey. He seemed to have to travel further and further each time.

She had to share everything with her younger brother and sister. They didn't seem to get picked on by the other little bears as much as Bea. Then again, they didn't love honey as much either. They seemed satisfied to eat fish. That just would not do for Bea; she had to have her honey.

Sometimes, Bea's little tummy was quite full of honey, and it kind of showed. She thought the honey must have moved down into her legs because they looked kind of full too. The other bears must have wished they could have as much honey to eat as she did. Or maybe they were just jealous because they didn't have a mom who loved them so much—a mom who would make sure there was lots and lots of honey for them anytime they wanted it, or a mom who did things to help them feel better when they were sad.

They were very, very mean to her. They called her a fat bear. She didn't understand what these words really meant, but from the way they growled and hissed and wrinkled up their noses, she knew it must be very bad. She felt awful. But she knew that even though they were not good to her, her mom was; she gave her honey to help her feel better.

This was the beginning of her "be good to myself" treat. This was good every time Bea had a problem to figure out. Even helpful if she was having a difficult time, was sad, frustrated, angry, tired, disappointed, or her fears were growing. She had honey when she was feeling happy. And each of these times she would have at least one pawful of honey. And usually, this required more than just one lonely pawful. But it truly was a great answer to any problem.

Chapter 10

THE DIRT PATH

B ea loved the adventure of going into untrod territory and actually finding her way back home. To get back to that lovely pine forest, she decided to take her new shortcut, the dirt path. The curious wee bear stopped short when she noticed the path had footprints on it. Could some other creatures have discovered this pathway too? The prints looked to be those of a wee bear going toward Bea's home.

To her memory, there had been no such creature. She tried her feet for size in the prints; they were her very own wee bear prints. How exciting to know the paw prints were still there even after she had left the path! More impressions were made in the soft dirt. Bea walked off the path for a distance and quickly returned to see if any prints were still there. They were.

She felt so proud to imagine others traveling along this path, coming upon her prints, and knowing they were the famous footprints of Bea the wee bear. She wondered if this path had a name; in her gleeful wee bear heart, it would from now on be named Bea's Golden Path.

This brought her so much happiness; the joyful bear returned time and time again. Sometimes, lots of jumbled markings were left by other creatures, who had finally happened upon her discovery. Other times, the playful whistling wind had erased them. This did not discourage Bea; this determined bear would keep coming back.

Chapter 11

SOMEONE CARING

You are finally going to meet Timothy, whom you have heard mentioned in many ways. Just as I was impressed, you will also be very impressed with everything about him. Timothy, an extremely important friend of Bea's, did the wood carving, clay pot making, and furniture building for her. He designed and carved the stepstooler and shelves for her honey clay pots, also made by him. Bea met Timothy on one of her strolling exercises. Besides helping her to be wee, we have surely seen how these exercises helped her to find and keep friends, which was so different from when she was younger.

These exercises brought her out of her cave, which at times was where she preferred to stay—in her dark, empty cave away from everyone, with her sad memories and her "be good to myself" treat. Venturing out, she always came back with a gift, whether it was a new seed to plant in her empty pots, the excitement of a newly discovered spot to do her brain exercises, or the nice memory of an encounter with a new friend.

Meeting Timothy was like discovering a very valuable treasure. Every time she spent time with him, she felt better and better about herself and her life. She had spent a lot of time worrying about her dear friends Scruffles and Sweet Puppy and helping them. This time it was her turn to have someone care about her, and Timothy certainly showed it. When a little voice inside her told her that she didn't deserve to have someone care about her, she remembered that time her mom told her that she was a good wee bear. She believed it now, after carrying the question with her for so many years

Scruffles had taught her that she was a good wee bear by the way he had come to love her over the years, purring so happily around her and sticking by her when she was very sad or scared. She knew that he really cared about her when he didn't run away if she nuzzled her face into his nice, soft fur to cry when she was sad. He always seemed to know when she was scared without her having to say it, for he stayed by her side rather than going by himself as independent cats often do.

Sweet Puppy seemed to be much more like Bea. She worried and didn't settle down very easily. She didn't seem to know what to do with or about her bad memories that would come rushing back without warning. Bea was certain that Puppy had nightmares even during the day. She would whine so mournfully in her sleep.

Unlike Scruffles, who was content to nibble on fish all day, Puppy seemed to want to eat all the time, a lot like Bea. And the times that would immediately come to Bea's memory were every time there were thunder and lightning storms; both of them would sit together in the back of the cave, with some of the flashes of lightning brightening the walls of their cave. They were no help to each other.

And Puppy was even frightened of lightning bugs! Bea guessed that Puppy thought they were lightning, even though Bea tried to convince her that they were nice little friends and would not hurt us. In fact, Bea loved lightning bugs. She loved the way they danced, lighting up the woods. They were so silent that she imagined what music they were making with a soft, rhythmic twinkling sound. She decided that it didn't seem like the right time to tell Sweet Puppy how delighted she was one time when about five of them entered the cave, lighting up the walls in very pretty designs.

She decided the best thing to ever say was that she would keep Puppy safe. In doing her notice exercise, she became aware that she seemed to worry more about Scruffles and Sweet Puppy than they did about her. And she hated to admit it to herself, but neither Scruffles nor Puppy were very reliable cuddlers. What a trio; they were all very wounded. She was to be the healer. Both Sweet Puppy and Scruffles had already had such terrible lives that Bea tried too darn hard to make things better for them, no matter what it took.

Sometimes, she did all the wrong things, which made everything worse, but she did them for the right reasons. Other times, she did the right thing, but probably for the wrong reason. She was trying to force a problem to come out the way she thought it should, not the way the maker knew would be best. She had changed since meeting Scruffles and Sweet Puppy. But with Timothy now in her life, caring about her, she would find her outlook on things and herself changing even more.

Chapter 12

STAND PROUD

On one of her strolling exercises, drawn to a newer path, Bea saw the possibility of a new friend off in the distance. Bea's mom taught her there are always possibilities, but sometimes you have to do the on-guard exercise and take the next step. Fears surely could return after having bad memories of those other mean little bears. As Bea carefully tiptoed toward her new sad friend, she began her brain exercise. Glancing around, the cautious wee bear saw no one else but herself—no furry friend like Scruffles to help her feel better.

When Bea asked her why she was so sad, she told Bea that she loved seeing children gather around her and hearing their laughter. Bea had to keep doing her brain exercise because she could not understand why that would make her friend sad. She guessed there must be more and that it had to do with fears. The wise bear knew she was right when her tall friend told her that the children hid sadness and fears in their deepest parts. She wanted to ask her weeping friend her name, but first she must remember the manners her mom had taught her. Asking politely, Bea learned her friend's name was Willow.

She remembered that she could do her talk to the maker of trees exercise to help her friend. As Bea moved a little to the side to do this, she noticed scar marks in Willow's bark. She was relieved they didn't look like beaver tooth marks. When Willow saw Bea's look of concern, she told Bea that the angry sticks held by the sad children had made those cuts. But she didn't mind if it helped them feel better.

Bea was surprised and, at the same time, thrilled that Willow must know about the maker too—the maker of trees and the maker of children. She told Willow that she understood the fears and how it felt like fifty bees were flying around inside her. She wondered if Willow felt like fifty termites were chewing around inside her. Willow said she was worried that she hadn't helped the children enough to give them hope. Bea did a little dance inside her brain to hear that Willow was worried too. She also understood that sinking feeling of trying to find hope, like she had to do when Bea's Golden Path turned black. Bea needed to do her brain exercise to help her friend find her hope again. She asked the maker of hope what to say. The maker told her to tell Willow that she held the memory for the children, so even if she still weeps, she should stand tall because it is a wonderful thing she does.

On her way back home, Bea felt a very warm, happy feeling and could not help but smile and thank the maker. As she continued her strolling exercise, she made sure she remembered the special markings on this path. She had learned so much from her new friend, Willow.

Chapter 13

A STRANGE
WARNING SMELL

There was a strange smell in the air, which warned Bea to do her strolling exercise in a new area. She had a very unsettled feeling in her tummy, far worse than the feeling of fifty bees swarming. It was more like what she might be feeling if, for some reason, she'd eaten a whole potful of bad honey that had suddenly turned black.

Tossing and twisting restlessly the whole night with that awful smell lurking, covering all other familiar smells, it was Bea's turn to tell her dear friend Scruffles the Raccoon Cat about her terrible dreams. She didn't fully understand what they meant but was certain they had something to do with Bea's Golden Path. Scruffles stayed by her bedside the entire night, comforting her and telling her he would go with her in the morning to help her make new footprints if something had happened to them.

The sun did not peek over the trees soon enough for Bea. Scruffles' eyes didn't seem to want to open; he was in a very deep sleep. Bea was so anxious that she didn't even take time for her "be good to myself" treat, nor would she allow Scruffles to do his morning cat bathing. Bea, usually a very patient wee bear, was aware of her impatience with Scruffles' slow, steady pace. She had a sense that something was terribly wrong and wanted to do sprinting rather than her usual strolling exercise.

Scruffles and Bea both changed their minds about making any new footprints and just stared at the ooze that covered the path that used to be called Bea's Golden Path. It wasn't gold anymore. It was black—the blackest black they had ever seen. And sadder yet, all of Bea's footprints were buried. All of the footprints of all of the creatures who had ever been privileged to tread upon Bea's Golden Path were somewhere here, underneath two inches of blacktop.

She told Scruffles that she was worried that someday all of the mud, topsoil, fallen pine needles, green grasses, and other unnamed dirt paths would be covered with blacktop. It was definitely time to do a very rigorous brain exercise. She decided to talk to the maker of the pine trees. She heard the comforting hum of the bees making honey and somehow knew that things would work out the way the maker knew would be best.

When a pine cone landed in front of her, she noticed a tiny pine tree that had sprouted up through a rock ledge. She smiled as she pictured pine trees and grasses breaking through this manmade blackness and all of the traces of creatures being rediscovered—best of all, the golden part of Bea's Golden Path.

Chapter 14

NO GOOD HOME

One of the most rigorous strolling exercises, which Bea the wee bear was on, had to come to a sudden halt. She saw the saddest sight she'd ever seen—sadder than Scruffy, sadder than Willow. Bea was wondering if she should do her investigation exercise. She remembered that sometimes she got her nose into sticky situations. She was quickly doing her scanning and planning. Those fifty bees were flying around inside her again. The fears were coming back. What big ears! She looked like she was part bat but without wings. Bea could tell this little one had been walking all alone forever with no "be good to myself" treats and no one to give them to her. There was no one to care for her.

After remembering her manners and introducing herself as Bea the wee bear, the puppy in front of her introduced herself as Bea the homeless puppy. What? Another Bea? What would she ever do? There could never be more than one Bea, unless it were the kind that makes her "be good to myself" treat. She smiled as she remembered the confusion when her mom would call her and the wrong bee would come.

She decided that she would name her "Sweet Puppy." Wow. Here she was again doing her very familiar trying to fix the unfixable exercise. This problem was much bigger than she could ever fix, even with her greatest imagination and pretending. Bea knew she needed to talk to the maker of puppies first. How could she and the maker help this forlorn, nearly hairless, stick-like creature in front of her? She had almost no hair on her hindquarters.

Once again, Bea realized she hadn't taken a breath and that she needed to remember to be alert but relaxed. She also had to help Sweet Puppy find hope. She did her brain exercise and read a poem to Sweet Puppy.

You look so sad.

I know your life has been so bad

I want to take you home,

so, you won't be alone

You'll never be so thin,

not after I've taken you in

Your name is Bea,

so, I know you're meant for me

You'll be a happy, happy puppy,

and meet my scruffy baby kitty

Scruffles now eats fish,

I will make sure to fill your dish

We can all sleep in one big room,

far away from any loud boom

Together, we will figure our problems out,

if you will just turn yourself about

Will you please come and live with us,

I'm sure there will be no big fuss

There was a terrible silence. And another silence followed, and then another. Bea wasn't sure she could stand the buzzing of the fifty bees flying around inside her. The fear was bigger than it ever had been. Just as she remembered how the maker had always helped her, a nice, comforting hum filled the air from busy bees making honey. She knew things would work out for all of them—Scruffles, Sweet Puppy, and Bea the wee bear.

Because Bea had been busy doing her brain exercises, she hadn't been doing her noticing exercise. She began to hear a whining sound. She wasn't sure if it was sad or a happy whining. But a skinny wagging tail told her that Sweet Puppy was going to say she would be happy to join Scruffles and her.

They could be seen walking toward home, moving from side to side as if doing a happy dance exercise.

Chapter 15

A TERRIBLE BOOM

Bea was once again very relieved to learn that puppies don't really like honey but do like fish; her "be good to myself" treat was safe. For this, she would gladly catch more fish. Just to make sure no fears would be growing and there would be enough fish, Bea did her talk to the maker of fish exercise.

Bea was surprised at how none of them really minded getting wet. Scruffles even played a bit trying to catch some minnows. Sweet Puppy did the "doggy paddle" in shallow water. This made her laugh harder than she had ever laughed before—a real bear belly laugh. Everyone got out and shook the water off as if they were shaking some of their bad memories off.

Sitting comfortably in their cozy home, Sweet Puppy told both Scruffles and Bea what she was so badly wanting to forget. The man she lived with yelled very loudly and slammed things around. He even made holes in the walls. She tried to distract the man when he went toward the woman by barking at him, but the man took his belt off and scared her so much that she went into her corner. Then the man threw her into a cold room, slammed the door, and left her there, where she shook all alone in the dark. She said she did not mind the darkness of the cave because it was different there. No one was going to hurt her, and there was no loud noise.

When Sweet Puppy said "loud noise," Bea had a bad memory of when she was very little. She was outside coloring in the sun with her mom. Gradually, her mom began to do her noticing exercise as the wind grew stronger. Bea's papers blew away from her purple crayon, as the treetops were bending more and more toward them. Her mom scooped her up as she leaped after her pages of hard work. Bea was surprised at how dark it had become in just those few moments. Her mom set her down as they entered their cave. She dropped her purple crayon, which she had been gripping, when there was a very loud, deafening boom. The fears started to grow as she remembered the next thing that happened. It doesn't seem real now. It couldn't have really happened.

But she knew it had, because every time she heard a loud boom, she would put her paws up over her head. That's what she wished she'd been able to do as the pieces of the ceiling of the cave came down on her head with a big branch sticking through an unwelcome big hole. There was more than a honeypot full of dirt covering her as her mom lovingly picked her up, brushed her off, and gave her a big mom bear hug. When they dared go outside, they found a very large elm tree had fallen on the roof of their home.

Ever since that time, Bea has not liked thunder and lightning storms. And that was what was happening right now. She wished Timothy the Beaver could be there with them. But beavers don't really like caves and want to be in the water way too much. He often sadly slapped his tail with one sound slap as she passed by. But she was still happy to see him, and he was happy to see her, and she would often find he'd left her several new pots, as he knew how often she might drop the empty ones. She did miss him so.

But this was not a time to do the distracted exercise. Sweet Puppy was beginning to shake more and more. Bea was afraid that if she didn't do her alert exercise soon, Sweet Puppy might have a heart attack. Her fears could not get in the way. And she had so many of them. She was conflicted about how to be able to see the lightning and be far enough away from the opening so that Sweet Puppy couldn't see it.

For Bea, counting after the lightning helped her know if the storm was coming closer or going away. She needed to remember how to count the way her mom had taught her. She knew the storm was getting closer if there were fewer numbers in her counting, and she was relieved when there were more numbers on this count after the last lightning flash.

Chapter 16

A REASON FOR RAINBOWS

Terrified when she saw lightning, Sweet Puppy knew a terrible boom was coming. Bea got them situated in the farthest corner of the cave. The only problem was that neither of them knew when the next terrible boom would come. They just sat there, clinging to each other.

Every once in a while, Sweet Puppy just had to peek out of the cave opening to see if there were any flashes of lightning, but would run right back, shaking. Just before Bea had time to do her talk with the maker of the lightning exercise, a loud, terrible boom made the whole cave shake. She had wanted to keep Sweet Puppy and herself safe. She had also included Scruffles, even though he didn't seem to be phased one bit by any of this.

He was actually sitting at the mouth of the cave. It was almost eerie to see his calm silhouette against the lit-up forest. He was definitely no help. Bea wanted someone to share in the trauma. She guessed it would always be just her and Sweet Puppy, who would be cowering in the safest, darkest corner of the cave.

She sat there shaking, with her "if onlys," "whys," and "no, it can't bes" Doing her notice exercise, she realized she was feeling very young, as if the tree had just come down on her cave again. She felt she was right back there, with the dirt covering her head. Her eyes were so tightly shut that she didn't see that Sweet Puppy was struggling against her clutching so tightly.

When she let up on her grip, her thoughts went to her great need for her "be good to myself" treat. If only she could get to it. She'd have just a little. Then, everything would be all better.

With doubts creeping in, she questioned her ability to keep anyone safe. But she knew that even though her fears were growing, she wasn't sure she could stand the buzzing of the fifty bees flying around inside her; she had to do her talk with the maker of lightning exercise.

She didn't know if the maker of thunder was the same as the maker of lightning, but she was pretty sure it was. So, she did her talk to the maker of everything exercise. Then, after a few quiet minutes, she heard a nice, comforting hum in the air of busy bees making honey, and she realized things would be okay.

For some reason, she knew that they could go back outside and maybe even see a rainbow. Scruffles was already sniffing the fresh air and had begun sunning himself to dry off. She did her notice exercise and saw that there was not just one rainbow but a double rainbow with all the colors so clear.

After doing her brain exercise, Bea had to admit that the maker of rainbows would not have been able to put that beautiful gift in the sky, wrapped in a double-striped ribbon, without the help of thunder, lightning, rain, and most importantly, the sun.

Chapter 17

NO BULLYING ALLOWED

Bea was pleased with how well Scruffles was treating Sweet Puppy. He was surprisingly welcoming, after all he was there first. There seemed to be no signs of jealousy or resentment from him. The new mom was concentrating in the wrong area, though. It was Sweet Puppy's behavior she needed to practice her notice exercise on. Scruffles had said nothing about how Sweet Puppy was bullying him.

It broke her wee bear mom's heart when it dawned on her what had been happening. Sweet Puppy was doing everything to make life miserable for Scruffles, who was finally feeling like life was calming down for him. Bea was no longer as happy as she had been, either. She watched as Sweet Puppy snaked over to Scruffles' food bowl and quickly gulped down his delectable meal of fish. Then she would approach her own filled bowl as if she knew nothing and appeared innocent. The discouraged mom had to refill Scruffle's empty bowl, dipping into the next meal's supply. This would mean they had to travel farther to find more fish. Their food supply was thinning out where they used to gather fish.

That was when Bea's eyes were open to more of Sweet Puppy's antics. Bea wondered if she had been deceived all along when she laughed to see them splashing each other. Doing her examination exercise, she realized it was Sweet Puppy who had been splashing Scruffles all along. Scruffles tried to get away from the forceful wave coming at him. He did love water, but the time for it and the amount of it needed to be done on his terms. Scruffles had been tolerant, but that was wearing very thin, and he felt like he was going to blow just like a worn tire on his former owner's truck.

It blew hard and was loud. The strangest sight was seeing how shredded the tire was. But Scruffles was beginning to feel like that tire, ready to blow and, at the same time, already shredded. Bea could feel the tension between those two growing. Sweet Puppy had a distinct grin that enraged both Scruffles and their desperate mom whenever she performed some of her deviant tricks.

Remember how Scruffles said he could not tolerate his old home life anymore and needed to take care of himself? As predicted, that frazzled raccoon cat began doing what he felt was the only way to take care of himself. Bea too often got caught in the carrying out of Scruffles' plan and had the wounds to prove it. As Sweet Puppy made her usual move to snatch up Scruffle's meal, with claws extended, he swiped her across the nose, the most vulnerable part of her body.

Neither Scruffles nor Bea had bargained for what happened next. A whole different side of Sweet Puppy came out, which forced Scruffles to respond as he had never needed to, even when he had to fight off other cats for the food in garbage cans.

Scruffles had never stood up for himself, certainly not to strike Sweet Puppy. This stunned Sweet Puppy, and because she no longer felt she had the upper paw, she became more snarly. This caused Scruffles to take a more aggressive stance. Sweet Puppy's lower-teeth grin changed to an upper-teeth snarl. As if a silent gun went off that only they could hear, they tore into each other.

Bea learned a hard lesson. Never get in between two angry animals. She felt puppy teeth snapping onto one arm, while the other was bitten and clawed. Her heart stung more than her arms. When they were fighting in the water, Bea got knocked down and could not get back up as they were fighting on top of her. She was sure she would be floating to the top if she could not get their weight off her. When she was finally able to get enough air to growl louder than they had ever heard her, this brought them to their senses. She told them how disgusted and angry she was. She pointed her paw at Sweet Puppy, telling her she was tempted to change her name.

She had changed Scruffles' name from Scruffy to Scruffles because he was improving; however, that was not the case with Sweet Puppy. The correcting mom attempted to shame Sweet Puppy, asking her why she thought she should still have the name "Sweet" as part of her name. Sweet Puppy put her head down and began whimpering. Bea was unable to tell if they were sincere tears. She demanded that Sweet Puppy admit to her bullying; just saying she was sorry was not enough. Bea knew how people can say they're sorry but not mean one word of what they're saying; it's just a way to avoid consequences.

She didn't know if Sweet Puppy might have learned the "I'm sorry" gimmick from her former family, so she was putting a stop to it before she thought she might get away with it. Scruffles might think it was sincere when it wasn't. It was very difficult for Sweet Puppy to name all of the bullying behaviors she had shown. Saying them aloud made her stop and think about why she had treated Scruffles in such a horrible way.

Scruffles had done nothing but be kind, helpful, and welcoming to her. Sweet Puppy promised herself she'd change back to the sweet puppy she was when she first joined this loving family. She would show them she was sincere.

Scruffles

Sweet Puppy

Chapter 18

A VALUABLE LESSON RECALLED

Bea knew if she got Sweet Puppy and Scruffles to work on a common project, their friendship would be strengthened. She had a perfect plan where everyone could benefit; they'd strengthen their loyalty to each other, and she would be able to add to her supply of honey, her be good to myself treat. The expedition was set; they would head out tomorrow to find the spots her mom had shown her to get good honey and plenty of it. Since it was such a long time ago, she hoped the tree would still be there. If not, that would make a big difference in their approach.

If something had happened to the designated tree, like the dear trees she'd seen burned badly by lightning, they would have to find the one, her mom had pointed out. Since that was earlier in her life, the location and the directions to it were quite foggy in her memory. She wasn't certain why everything in that period of her life was an absolute blur. She could remember nothing about it. She feared it might all come rushing back if they had to hunt down that second tree.

Bea, their mom, instructed Scruffles and Sweet Puppy that there was to be no quarreling. That uncalled-for behavior would alarm and disturb the bees, and that would not do. She reviewed with them what her mother had told her about bees who had black on their heads. She cautioned them to avoid disturbing them. They agreed and began their strolling exercise. It seemed like no time before Bea announced that they had reached the honey tree. Sweet Puppy saw movement under a branch and began using her nose to nuzzle into the dried grass under the fallen, decaying limb.

When Sweet Puppy dove at Scruffles and knocked him to the ground, both Bea and Scruffles were disappointed to see that the old, unacceptable behavior had returned. Bea was just about to redirect Sweet Puppy when the alert puppy explained that she had seen a black-headed bee zooming toward Scruffles to sting him. Bea was increasingly skeptical of this explanation when Sweet Puppy knocked Scruffles down again. Sweet Puppy, not Scruffles, yelped, yowled, and meowed. Sweet Puppy had been stung.

Regaining his balance, Scruffles recognized that Sweet Puppy had been protecting him with the tackle. What a pleasant surprise for Bea! They both went to hug Sweet Puppy, being careful not to touch her wounded shoulder. Scruffles repeatedly thanked Sweet Puppy, who admitted that she was the one who stirred the mean bees up by moving the log.

As they stood away from the log, they could see the nest, crawling and angrily buzzing with more mean bees.

The mean bees had taken over the whole tree. The three honey tree searchers would be safer if they stepped far away. It seemed the message from the good bees was that they had moved. Bea said it seemed that one bee had waited and waited for that one moment when he got the signal to sting the one who disturbed their branch and nest or anyone who was around there.

There was going to be a stretch for Bea to tap into the old, dusty memory to lead them to where the other tree was. She wondered why she could not remember. What happened then that she was blocking? She did her brain exercise and talked to the maker. She had to trust in the results of those exercises. The contented bear was encouraged that everything would be all right when she heard the inner signal of peace with the humming of bees making honey.

She felt as if she'd been struck by lightning when they found themselves in a broad field, surrounded by a fence with trees in the background. Scruffles and Sweet Puppy did not understand what was happening, nor what they could do to stop their mom from falling to the ground, shaking and sobbing. They looked helplessly at each other. It seemed that their mom was the only one who could do anything about whatever was going on with her. They'd never seen her so broken.

When she caught her breath and did her talk to the maker and her be calm exercise, she made the same choice her mom had those many rainy times ago. She would never tell them what horrors she saw in that wooden building. She hoped this was the moment she could get beyond that terrible experience, just as she had so many other dark times when it didn't feel like the sun would ever shine in her heart.

The wee bear did her brain exercise to remember what she had done in the past to change the pictures in her head. The sound of the music from the trees came back to her. The colors spun into lovely, hopeful patterns. Her heart was filled with music, and she began dancing, matching the colors with different feelings. The yellows were like the bright, cheery sun. The reds reminded her of what her mom told her was the color of love and friendship. The oranges were the color of the sun when it was resting and preparing to sleep for the night to wake up the next morning to light the day. The brown was the color of her soft fur, which wrapped a precious wee bear in warmth and love and complete acceptance.

The maker of these leaves and her love for trees told her it was time to put those horrible memories of what she saw in that wooden building back where they belonged. Those events were similar to other dark times when she was little, like being bullied by the mean little bears and her fear that when the wind gets angry, it might make a branch fall onto her cave home. She was no longer little; in addition, she was a mom who had to take care of a raccoon cat and a sweet puppy. She could be happy for the first time, maybe ever. As she looked around, her heart was filled with the colors of the leaves.

It was time to go to the tree that her mother had pointed out to her. The dark cloud in her memory was gone. The fear had vanished. She knew exactly where that tree was growing. That wise bear was certain they would find the kind bees living there, making honey, her "be good to myself" treat.

Chapter 19

BEA'S WISDOM

One thing Bea the wee bear doesn't have any trouble sharing is the wisdom she has received from the maker of bees. She has found much wisdom in her honeypots during some of her exercises. She had gotten pretty good at doing her brain exercise and fine motor weightlifting at the same time, which simply means she could figure things out while enjoying her "be good to myself" treat.

One time, when she thought there was no honey left in any of her honeypots, she decided it was time to do her investigation exercise. Using her wee nose, she looked inside each empty pot to see if there might be just enough to do a few more fine motor weightlifting exercises.

She found that the pots were not empty after all. They were not full of honey, but were filled with something almost better for a wee bear—

one who was deciding whether or not to get involved in someone's problems.

There were all kinds of wisdom to be found while searching through each honeypot. It turned out to be a meditation exercise, where Bea at first thought of nothing other than the inside of each empty pot. Because there is nothing to distract her except the emptiness of the pot, her mind can be empty and then become filled with wisdom.

Bea may not always have understood what wisdom means, but she surely knows how it has helped answer many, many questions. It's a kind of "just knowing something." As she sat doing her brain exercise, she got an idea, then another, and another. Each pot, as she stuck her nose into it, became filled with an answer to her question.

She was afraid that one particular pot would be filled with her wee bear nose when she got a little too deep into her investigation exercise and got her nose stuck. She then had to do her "detaching from things that have a hold on you" exercise. We have seen time and time again that Bea has struggled to use this wisdom. She can't seem to remember what can happen when someone gets their nose stuck in very uncomfortable places that are not meant for them. The place could be a clay pot of honey or, in this case, someone else's business.

Sometime before meeting her dear friend Scruffles the Raccoon Cat, she was feeling very lonely and wanted to understand more about being lonely. She decided to talk to the maker of the bees, who understands when Bea has too much or too little. Bea realized that being lonely is like her honeypots when they no longer have any honey left. Yes, that's it; she gets an empty feeling—a very, very empty feeling, with a hollow sound echoing all around inside her as if the fifty buzzing bees have left and there is only emptiness.

She stills herself and does her brain exercise, and she thinks about how to get beyond moments of loneliness. This is similar to how she might go about solving her problem when her honeypots are empty. If she were to stroll to a friend's to ask for some honey, she might get to their door and there'd be no answer. She might know of a place they'd said a key would be left, such as under the mat. What would happen if she found no key there or if some of her friends lived in places fairly inaccessible to Bea? The doors might be too small, too high, or too deep in the ground. What would she do?

One of the problems in this plan of Bea's is that if she did by chance find someone home, she, unfortunately, would have difficulty holding herself back from asking them for all of their honey. This behavior would go against any manners her mother taught her. She would instantly wear out her welcome. Somehow, she could never bring herself to do things in moderation. Ah, that was just another exercise on her list that she could definitely begin to practice. And if she stopped to consider her friends' needs, she would realize that she would be leaving them with only empty pots. No one would be any better off. Soon, her newly acquired honey would be gone. She'd be holding only empty honeypots again. The other thing she could do is just sit and do nothing and stay hungry and miserable.

But the best, most productive, and most rigorous exercise she could do was to go in search of her favorite honey tree. Just like going to search for honey in uncertain places, she needs to find the friend that she knows is really going to be there for her. Only she can solve her loneliness problem. We have seen this proven with her enriching relationships with Timothy. And of course, she knows that her two best cave mates, Scruffles and Sweet Puppy, will do the best they can.

She is suggesting that we do this rigorous brain exercise in particular, among all others. Even though it is very rigorous, it can be very effective in helping us realize that we are all like her honeypots. Sometimes it is full, but sometimes it is empty. Sometimes lonely. Sometimes not. That's just the way of things.

Chapter 20

CRASHING SOUNDS

Often, while rearranging her honeypots, Bea would do her brain exercises. During these quiet moments, she would remember to thank the beaver's maker, especially the talented woodcarving beavers. She believed that the maker had sent Timothy to paddle into her life for many wonderful reasons. He was, first and foremost, a woodcarver. As time passed, he began to carve more and more furniture for her humble cave. The very handsome cupboard that held her most precious honeypots, the very sturdy stepstool that she used for her rigorous exercise program, and the very ornate clay pots were all made by him.

One time, when she was vigorously doing her stepstooling and weight-lifting, the weights got too tippy and went crashing to the floor. She was so upset that she immediately stopped all of her other exercises and began her on-guard exercise; her fears were back. She didn't exactly understand why she was feeling so unsafe but had an idea it had to do with when she was little and others used to call her clumsy bear.

Because she was so focused on not being criticized, her fears got in the way of her thinking, and she forgot to do her notice exercise and stumbled over a root hidden by the thick, soft layer of pine needles. It's a good thing it was a very thick blanket because she landed hard. But what hurt the most was the belittling laughter.

What could she ever tell Timothy? She frantically began her trying to fix the unfixable exercise. She tried to glue the pieces back together with honey. Her "be good to myself" treat had helped with many other problems in the past, but not this time. The jagged pieces would not hold together well enough to look like the clay pot it used to be or to even look like any clay pot.

She felt like a fragile, cracked pot, ready to fall apart and never be put back together again. She jaggedly remembered that one of the glues of a good friendship is honesty. She did her talk to the maker of truth exercise. After a very quiet moment, she was sure she heard the gentle slapping of water. She knew somehow things would work out for both of them.

She immediately set off for Timothy's Pond. She found him busily planting some new young trees, which he had started with acorns and seeds from pine cones that she and he had gathered over time. When she cautiously and trustingly told him what had happened, he smiled—not a sneer as she was so used to, but a "knowing" smile. Did Timothy have wisdom, too?

He began to tell her of the many, many, many clay pots he had broken, or perhaps a better word would be demolished. You see, after he had finished making a nice line of clay pots and had left them to dry in the sun, he decided to cut some trees. You guessed it. And not just one tree came crashing down on the newly dried pots! And not only that time, either.

When others might get very upset about serious things, Timothy the Talented Beaver had such a wonderful way of making them seem almost funny. Bea had never been able to laugh and take things so lightly before meeting Timothy. If there were a way to know when a bear smiles, you would be able to see the widest and most contented smile on Bea the wee bear's face. She knew that she was certainly smiling in her heart, anyway. Another fact that put her mind at ease was that beavers did not care for honey; their most favorite food was tree bark.

Now, Bea may have snacked on some fine grasses when no honey was available, but never on tree bark—that she could remember. Timothy did not have such an easy time getting at it. The best and most tender bark was at the top of the hardwood trees, and since he couldn't climb way up here, he regretfully had to cut down a lot of trees. One of the reasons he made sure to plant some new ones was that he was concerned that someday there wouldn't be any trees left, and he did not want to be responsible for that. Bea had an excellent idea.

Chapter 21

CLIMBING HIGH

Beavers can't climb trees, but wee bears can. Timothy, the talented beaver, thought her idea was excellent too. Now he could go about the job of choosing the right trees to fell for carving and building his dam and canals. Best of all, he would be able to upgrade his home, which he calls a lodge.

Up the tree, Bea went. First, she only climbed in her mind. She had actually never climbed a tree in reality. She heard bears could do it. So now her pretending and not being absolutely honest were giving her some consequences. She wasn't even sure how to start, but, with great trepidation, she soundly dug her sharp claws on her hind paws as high up on the tree as she could. Then, she quickly dug in with her front claws so as not to tip over backward. There would be no cushion of comfy pine needles to land on.

She talked to the maker all the way up and remembered not to look down at Timothy, not even to see if he was smiling, had a worried look in his kind eyes, or trusted her and was going about his scheduled tasks. She somehow made it to the very top, where those tender shoots grow.

She broke off as many as she could, so she might never have to do that again. As she let them drop one by one, her fears started to grow. How would she ever get back down to safe ground? Talking to the maker helped her with her brain exercise. Who would ever have thought she'd be doing her brain exercise at the top of a tree!

Somehow, she figured out how to go back down, one step at a time, by thinking backwards. As long as Bea knows what thinking backwards means, that's all that counts. That was an adventure that she would never forget. Timothy was so pleased and proud of her for her bravery. That fact almost made it worth it. In addition to learning how to climb up and then climb down a very tall tree, Bea learned several other things:

1. Don't act like you know something when you don't have any idea what you're talking about at all.

2. Don't offer to do something until you have done your investigation exercise.

3. Don't do something if you don't have confidence in yourself for the task. Getting very hurt is not going to build your confidence.

4. Take care of yourself before you try to take care of someone else.

5. Do remember that when you put yourself in a dangerous situation to kind of rescue a person in their needs, that person most probably could and would figure something else out.

At this point, Bea was tired of learning and talking about it. She just wanted to forget it all for a while and enjoy her life. But that always seemed short-lived. Bea did a lot of laughing with Timothy because he told a lot of funny stories about things that had happened to him.

But sometimes he seemed to get sad and would talk about something that happened to him when he was younger that was not funny. As they strolled down some of the best paths, Bea had begun finding good seeds or little saplings for Timothy to plant. As you may know, Beavers favor the hardwood trees. Often, they would walk about looking at how the little trees were doing, feeling so good about everything.

But sometimes he seemed to get sad and would talk about something that happened to him when he was younger that was not funny. As they strolled down some of the best paths, Bea had begun finding good seeds or little saplings for Timothy to plant. As you may know, Beavers favor the hardwood trees. Often, they would walk about looking at how the little trees were doing, feeling so good about everything.

On one such occasion, Timothy was quiet for a moment but then began telling Bea of a time when he was younger and how he had planted many, many trees like this on a nice plot of land. He told of how good he felt about himself and his life, unlike his beaver brother, who always seemed unhappy but never did anything about it.

One late afternoon, while resting after a very busy Beaver Day, he heard a very strange sound. When he went to investigate, to his horror, he saw his beaver brother's friend, the greedy goat, crunching on his new struggling saplings. His heart sank at the sound, and worse yet, his jealous brother was watching the whole time. Pine trees grow very quickly and make a great screen to hide the good trees. But either the goat didn't care or the pine trees were not able to grow fast enough.

Bea loves Timothy even more now. He also had bad memories. just like Willow, Scruffles, Sweet Puppy, and, of course, Bea herself. She hoped so much that he would often talk to the maker, but of course she would never ask. She somehow thought he did talk to the maker of everything. She didn't know why, but it just seemed that he did.

WAITING

After spending time with Timothy and his little growing trees and after doing some brain exercises, Bea has come to look at many things in a different way. When she stays home, she has all kinds of friends come to visit her in all kinds of weather.

She always hopes that they are bringing a little of her "be good to myself" treat. This will probably never change. But on rainy days, besides pots of honey and colorful umbrellas, they bring dark clumps of mud. Bea has heard a lot of complaints and apologies about mud from different creatures.

In one of her brain exercises, she got the wisdom to know that the maker of rain would not have made mud if it weren't good for something. After all, Timothy uses it to make pots. The nuisance about mud seems to be that it gets on paws or claws, then drops off on different areas of the floor or on furniture.

Because mud is damp or wet, the complainers have to wait for it to dry, then sweep it up and throw it back outside—only for it to turn into mud again during the next rainfall, to be tracked in again, to be swept up, and to be tracked in again. Bea calls this a senseless exercise—not one she would want to practice.

She is sure there are better and more sensible things to do with mud than sweep it up and track it back in. She has noticed that a lot of the mud comes from the top of the ground, so it must have good topsoil in it. After her generous mud-donating friends have left and she has made sure she has done her fine motor weightlifting, she gets out her straw broom and wooden dustpan, carved by Timothy.

Watching Timothy had given her a great idea. She would plant seeds of all kinds that she had found during her little, rigorous strolling exercises. She would plant them in her empty pots, of which she sadly has many. Empty is never good.

Soon there would be green and colorful things growing all over her home. Taking them outside for rain and sun, she is very kind to these plants and places them in the southern opening of her cave, for she knows that most plants love the southerly exposure.

She also knows that waiting for seeds to grow is a better exercise than the tired waiting others do when they are waiting for the mud to dry and thinking terrible thoughts about the mud, whose mud it is, and the time they are spending waiting for it to dry.

Waiting for a seed to sprout or a flower to grow doesn't feel like waiting. She thinks this is a good time to busy herself with her "Be Wee with Bea" exercises, taking time out, of course, for her "be good to myself" treat. Many of these seedlings will be perfect for Timothy, too.

Chapter 23

A GOOD LAUGH

A new friend who came to visit more and more was a cat that Bea remembered was named Harriet. Bea didn't say anything to Scruffles but made a plan in her mind, as she was so often prone to do regarding Scruffles—scanning and planning. As her plans, as you may remember, don't always work out the way Bea wants them to, but the way the maker thinks is best.

Bea was enjoying her special friendship with Timothy and knew how much happier she was now. It's not that she was unhappy before, but it felt good to be thought of by Timothy as special.

She knew that Scruffles certainly was not unhappy but could always be happier, as any of us could. She encouraged Scruffles to get out more, hoping to herself that he would run into Harriet. She did some of her on-guard exercises when she saw them playfully chasing and dancing each other around.

She made sure that no other creature disturbed them. Bea would sometimes dance a little too. She had become a very practiced dancer. She was very happy when Harriet would come over to visit Scruffles, fixing them some "be good to myself" treats—fish that she caught in her favorite fishing spot.

She got such enjoyment watching them sunning themselves together. She could tell Scruffles looked forward to seeing Harriet. After a few days had passed with no sign of Harriet, Bea began to worry. As we know, she worried about those she cared about. A week later, part of the mystery was solved. Harriet must have been very injured by a car or other animal.

She must not have been able to get to see Scruffles. Harriet was probably nursing her wounded leg. The terrible redness of her flesh was only beginning to heal. Bea wondered also if another bully cat had hurt her the way Orion and Sam had hurt Scruffles, but this looked different. She was so glad that Harriet felt a desire to visit Scruffles in spite of her needing to heal further.

Bea had learned a little from her investigation exercises, which, as you may remember, ended up with her nose in a very sticky situation. But, as you might imagine, that was not enough, and she was about to get quite a surprise and have quite a laugh—a bear belly laugh.

She had been doing all of the minding of someone else's business exercises. But this time, it was only in her head, so she felt this was quite an improvement. But she was still scanning and planning. She could stand it no longer. She had to ask Scruffles how things were going between him and Harriet.

When she said "Harriet," he looked very puzzled. Bea told him how she had been enjoying watching him and Harriet play together. Having been around Timothy and his laughter, Bea did not feel hurt but puzzled when Scruffles laughed. She had to laugh at herself too. She was beginning to have a sense of humor for the first time in her whole wee bear life.

That was going to become another "Be Wee with Bea" exercise in her program, which had developed into quite a lengthy list. Not taking herself so seriously had given her more opportunity to do her notice exercise—to notice the beauty around her and never forget to thank the maker of everything.

In answer to her question, he said, "My friend's name is Ozzie, not Harriet." And we will leave it at that, only to take a moment to imagine the lessons Bea could have learned from this incident.

Chapter 24

BEING WEE

As we have strolled along with Bea the wee bear, she has found exercises that have helped her solve problems. Some might say she is a great success. She must have some magic formula to be able to live as happily as she does. This is true even though things do not always go the way she wishes they would. She has gotten one very important bit of wisdom from the maker of the seed of a mustard flower. Looking at the center, we can see the seed is so very, very wee. Bea's lesson is about how to be wee and yet be thought very, very great by the maker, just like that seed.

You see, she doesn't really very often think of life as a problem, as long as she remembers to talk to the maker. We've noticed many times when she's forgotten to do that. But when she finally did her "talk to the maker" exercise, she calmed down, and things worked out as they were supposed to.

We have seen how, at first, Bea thought she needed to fix every problem she saw. But in learning to be wee, she has found a new way to be happy. We are not just talking about her wishing that she had a wee body. No, being wee has come to mean so much more to Bea. Whenever she talks to the maker to ask for help solving big, big problems, she realizes she is wee. She realizes she cannot make anything go right without the help of the maker.

Did you notice that she never named herself Bea the Great Bear, not even when she was talking about her paw prints on Bea's Golden Path? She did not really understand what the word "humble" meant, but the maker asked her to do a humble exercise. This simply meant that she would take time out of her other exercises to thank the maker of all things for any and all of the gifts she has discovered. Especially the music all around her, and of course, her friends, and her ability to breathe when she remembered.

Being wee also meant that she listened to all things, to hear the message the maker wanted her to hear. She learned that as long as she remembered to be wee, she would be great. This sometimes confused her, but she had learned not to question the ways of the maker of all things, and especially the maker of wee bears.

I wanted you to meet Bea, to walk along Bea's Golden Path, to do some of her rigorous exercises, to discover some of her wisdom, and to learn to listen to all the living things around you. Don't forget the rocks; they just might have something to teach you. But, most of all, I hope that by meeting Bea the wee bear, you have learned to be wee with Bea.

The End

...for now

Glossary

BRAIN EXERCISE

Serious thinking and/or meditation

STROLLING

Walking with great alertness

STEPSTOOLING

Going up and down a step stool to get clay pots of honey

FINE MOTOR WEIGHT LIFTING

Using the paw to lift gobs of honey from the pot to the mouth

TOE TOUCHING

Not wanting to waste a drop of honey, bending over to earnestly clean the gooey toes

FLOOR TOUCHING

Similar to toe touching except having to bend over further, to the floor

BULLY

To taunt, call names, belittle by laughing, exclude from activities, and emotionally pushy, often resulting in long-term trauma and emotional scarring

NOTICE EXERCISE

Really focus on what is in front of you, to really see things as they are, all done without distraction; a good way to clear the mind

PLANNING AND SCANNING

A little bit of plotting to figure out how to solve someone's problem that is basically unsolicited, this often ends up badly

STUCK

Unable to move on; fixated on an idea or situation or problem

FEARS

A form of anxiety, often resulting from trauma from a painful or frightening incident or bullying

TRYING TO FIX THE UNFIXABLE EXERCISE

A form of denial, lack of acceptance of situations as they are

HUMBLE EXERCISE

Very important for progress, needing to think of others rather than just oneself, to be grateful, not unnecessarily self-important, yet recognizing and admitting one's own strengths, a balance comes to exist

PRETENDING

Not being totally honest with oneself or others, it is often a learned form of lying and maybe unconsciously done, sometimes done to take care of another's feelings

This book is about learning healthy ways to cope.

and how to help others to cope.

If you've been bullied

If you have anxiety

If you need to solve problems

If you worry about your looks

It teaches how to find hope and give hope

Recommended

Independent Readers

4-6 grades